For Dack and Danielle Nehring:
family helps us weather all storms. —L.P.S.

To Dad, who loves a good thunderstorm. —E.M.

**BLOOMSBURY CHILDREN'S BOOKS**
Bloomsbury Publishing Inc., part of Bloomsbury Publishing Plc
1385 Broadway, New York, NY 10018

**BLOOMSBURY, BLOOMSBURY CHILDREN'S BOOKS,** and the Diana logo are
trademarks of Bloomsbury Publishing Plc

First published in the United States of America in March 2023
by Bloomsbury Children's Books

Text copyright © 2023 by Laura Purdie Salas
Illustrations copyright © 2023 by Elly MacKay

Bloomsbury Publishing Plc does not have any control over, or responsibility for,
any third-party websites referred to or in this book. All internet addresses given
in this book were correct at the time of going to press. The author and publisher
regret any inconvenience caused if addresses have changed or sites have ceased to
exist, but can accept no responsibility for any such changes.

Bloomsbury books may be purchased for business or promotional use. For
information on bulk purchases please contact Macmillan Corporate and Premium
Sales Department at specialmarkets@macmillan.com

Library of Congress Cataloging-in-Publication Data
available upon request

ISBN 978-1-5476-0225-4 (hardcover) · ISBN 978-1-5476-0226-1 (e-book) ·
ISBN 978-1-5476-0227-8 (e-PDF)

The art in this book was created three dimensionally with layers of paper.
Lightning and rain was added in Procreate.
Typeset in Sasson Sans Std
Book design by Jeanette Levy
Printed in China by Leo Paper Products, Heshan, Guangdong
2 4 6 8 10 9 7 5 3 1

To find out more about our authors and books visit www.bloomsbury.com
and sign up for our newsletters.

# ZAP! CLAP! BOOM!

## THE STORY OF A THUNDERSTORM

Laura Purdie Salas

illustrated by Elly MacKay

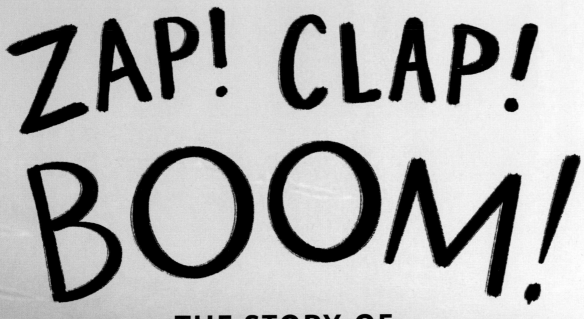

BLOOMSBURY
CHILDREN'S BOOKS
NEW YORK  LONDON  OXFORD  NEW DELHI  SYDNEY

Sunny day sits warm and dry.
No wind,
no rain,
no stormy sky.

Morning's calm.
Outside is still.
A blue-forever day,

until . . .

Warmer air                                     begins to                                     rise,

floating up
toward cooler skies.

Clouds of fluffy, puffy white.
Pillows billow,
soft
and light.

Starting low,
they grow
and grow—
white above,
now gray below.

Rustling,
murmuring
rush begins
of whispering leaves
in newborn
winds.

No rain yet.
It's just a threat—
a rising cloud,
a towering plume,

then . . .

Flicker, flitter, skitter, flash!
Pounding
sounding distant
crash!

Sky is churning.
Breeze blows stronger.
Dry for now,
but not much longer.

Clouds hang heavy,
black, and dark.
Smudgy watercolor mark.

They hover over,
tower,
loom,

then . . .

Swollen clouds begin to drain,

spilling
splashing,
chilling
rain.

Wind blows fiercely,
howls
and shrieks.
The world
groans slowly,
shivers,
creaks.

Bolts of lightning
flare
and scare.
Electric zigzags
slice the air.

Thunder rumbles.
When it comes,
it rolls,
it stomps,
it rattles,
drums.

A crackling, grumbling
sound of doom,

then . . .

ZAP!
CLAP!
BOOM!

Sky falls quiet.
Not a sound.
No rain slamming on the ground.

Earth was washed
by water pressure.

Now it's
dazzling,
sparkling,
fresher.

Diamond drops
dress trees and vines.
Storm is over.

**The world now shines.**

# THE SCIENCE BEHIND STORMS

I grew up in Florida, and many summer afternoons followed a pattern. The sky darkened, thunder rumbled, lightning flashed, and rain poured. We kids stopped swimming, canoeing, or playing kickball and dashed inside. An hour later, the skies cleared, leaving sunshine and a puddled ground behind. These storms were impressive, and fascinating, too. I wondered, what made them happen? Where did they get their power?

## HERE COMES THE RAIN

The real beginning of a thunderstorm happens long before the first raindrop falls. Huge air masses are always forming over the Earth, and these masses each have their own temperature and moisture level. You can think of an air mass like a giant bubble of air.

When winds blow them around, these air masses sometimes bump into each other. If a hot air mass and a cold air mass collide, the hot air mass rises. Warmer air always rises because it's lighter than colder air. As the hot air rises, the water vapor in the air mass condenses into water droplets and forms a cumulus cloud—white, puffy, and low in the sky.

As warm air continues to float up from the ground, more water droplets form, and the cloud grows. When it reaches 20,000 feet high, it becomes a cumulonimbus cloud. You might see one cumulonimbus cloud all by itself, dark and threatening. Or cumulonimbus clouds might fill the sky. Each cloud can be several miles wide and more than 70,000 feet tall!

The warm air flowing upward keeps all those water droplets aloft in the sky. But sometimes a cloud becomes so large and heavy that the air flow can't hold the water droplets up anymore. When that happens, look out! It's raining!

## LIGHTING UP THE SKY

Lightning is the flashiest part of a thunderstorm. From Earth, we see just a small fraction of all the lightning that's created. The most common types of lightning usually flash so high up that they're invisible to us on the ground. Those types are intra-cloud lightning, which happens inside one cloud, and cloud-to-cloud lightning, which happens between two clouds. The lightning we almost always see is a third kind: cloud-to-ground lightning.

All lightning is electricity. Although scientists still don't know exactly how lightning forms, they do know it can form only when a positive charge meets a negative charge.

The water droplets at the bottom of a thundercloud provide the negative electric charge for cloud-to-ground lightning. It's almost as if these negative charges are calling, "Come here, positive charges!" Then, positive charges in the ground itself travel up into the tallest objects around—like trees, towers, or buildings. When the negative charges are strong enough, an electric current shoots down from the cloud, searching for a pathway to the ground. This part of the lightning races downward at 200,000 miles per hour—too fast for us to see.

But as that strand of electricity barrels toward Earth, another strand reaches up *from* the Earth to meet it. ZAP! *That* is the lightning we can easily see. If one strand reaches up, you see one solid lightning bolt. If several strands reach up from Earth, you see forked lightning.

# BOOM!

Thunder is a side effect of lightning. Lightning is hot—around 54,000 degrees Fahrenheit! The air around the lightning heats and expands so quickly that shock waves ripple through the atmosphere. CLAP! We hear those shock waves as thunder. BOOM!

Eventually, the drama and noise of a thunderstorm end. As water in the cloud empties out, air starts moving down instead of up. These downward drafts of air carry the higher, cooler air out of the clouds. That stops warm air from being carried upward, and the cloud stops growing. At this point, the sky quiets and the storm ends—and kids can run back outside to play again.

The next time nature puts on a dramatic thunder and lightning show, find a cozy spot near a window and watch the storm unfold.

## SELECTED SOURCES

Paul Douglas, in conversation with Laura Purdie Salas,
email correspondence from December 6, 2018 to May 4, 2022.

"Thunderstorm Basics," NOAA National Severe Storms Laboratory,
National Oceanic and Atmospheric Administration, accessed March 8, 2018,
https://www.nssl.noaa.gov/education/svrwx101/thunderstorms/

"Thunderstorm FAQ," NOAA National Severe Storms Laboratory,
National Oceanic and Atmospheric Administration, accessed March 8, 2018,
https://www.nssl.noaa.gov/education/svrwx101/thunderstorms/faq/

"Life Cycle of a Thunderstorm," US Department of Commerce, NOAA. NWS JetStream,
NOAA's National Weather Service, accessed September 12, 2019,
https://www.weather.gov/jetstream/life

## FOR FURTHER EXPLORATION

**Websites:**
NOAA SciJinks – All About Weather: scijinks.gov
National Geographic: nationalgeographic.org/topics/resource-library-weather/
Center for Science Education: scied.ucar.edu/learning-zone/storms/thunderstorms

**Time-Lapse Videos:**
Mike Olbinski, YouTube: youtube.com/c/MikeOlbinski
Nicolaus Wegner, Vimeo: vimeo.com/nicolauswegner

**Books:**
*Tap Tap Boom Boom* by Elizabeth Bluemle and G. Brian Karas
*A Party for Clouds: Thunderstorms* by Belinda Jensen, Renée Kurilla, and Lisa Bullard
*National Geographic Kids Ultimate Weatherpedia* by Stephanie Warren Drimmer
*Blue on Blue* by Dianne White and Beth Krommes

With gratitude to meteorologist and author Paul Douglas for his time, expertise, and enthusiasm in reading this manuscript and answering my questions.